Write in the missing letters of the alphabet on the boots.

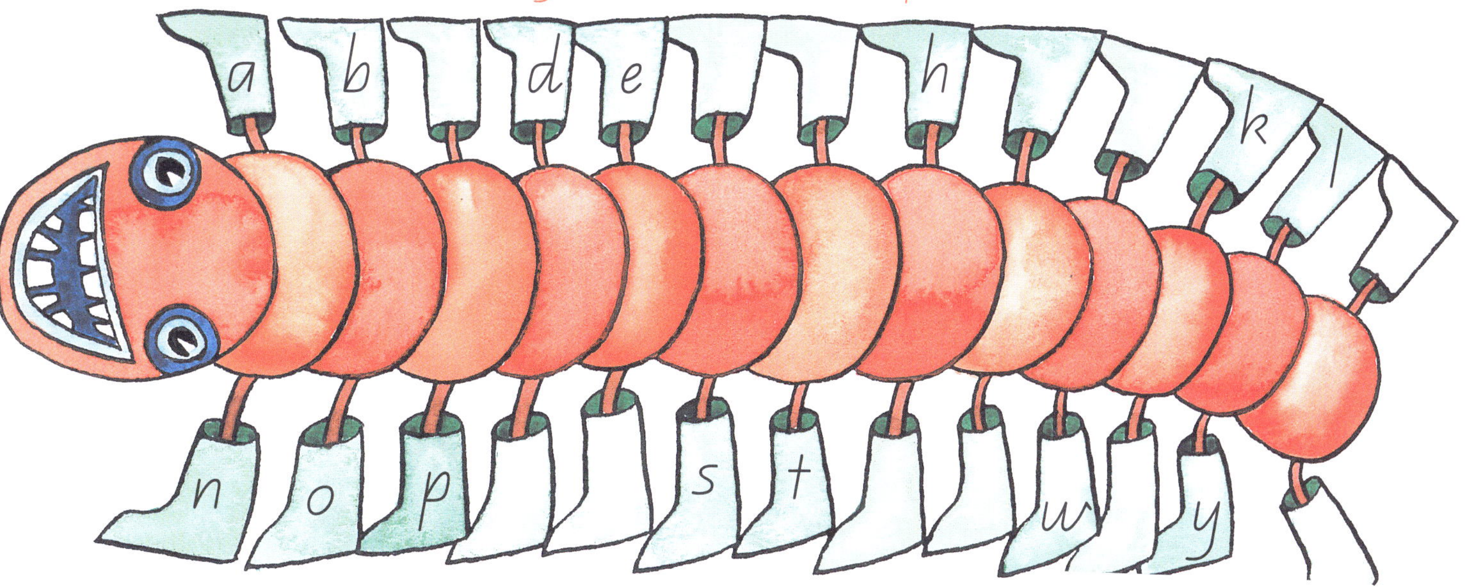

My name is ________________________

CONTENTS

INTRODUCTION

The current Queensland handwriting script was introduced over several years from 1985, after a successful trial. Its print style, the Beginner's Alphabet, is based on simple, italic cursive shapes that are easily joined to become Queensland Modern Cursive. Because capitals remain the same, the two scripts merge easily, so children find cursive writing much easier to write as well as read. Queensland Modern Cursive is designed to be fluent and quick, with maximum legibility.

FOCUS

This book contains a carefully sequenced handwriting program for children in Year One:

- pre-writing patterns based directly on letter shapes
- introduction of letters on a base line in rotation groups
- forming lower-case letters on single sets of red and blue lines in colour-coded spatial groups
- forming capital letters on red and blue lines in alphabetical order
- consolidation of all letters through meaningful sentences.
- Theme: fairytales.

TECHNIQUE

Pencil grip

1. The thumb and the index finger support the pencil while it rests on the middle finger.
2. Child should be able to tap the pencil with the pointer finger while it is supported by the middle finger and thumb.
3. There should be a distance of approx. 2–2.5 cm from the pencil point to the tip of the index finger, 3 cm for a left-hander. Triangular pencil-grips promote correct finger placement and distance.

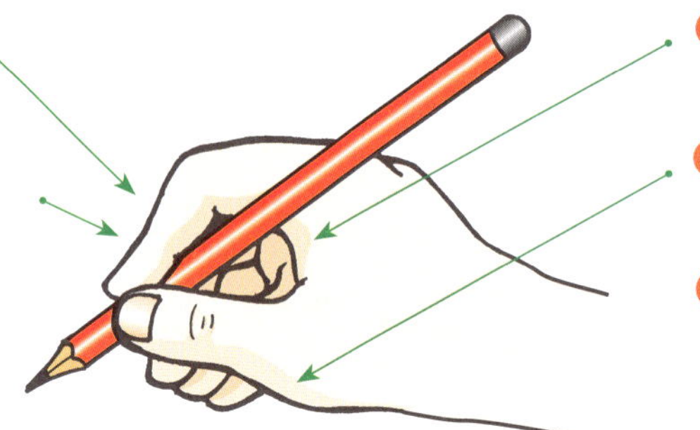

4. Hold pencil barrel up high, near or before the knuckle. Pencil should not rest low in the "web" of the hand.
5. The side of the hand and the little finger act as supports for the whole hand.
6. Unpainted pencils are less slippery.

Posture

Right-handers

1. Keep back straight at an angle of about 30° to back of chair, and keep bottom towards back of seat.

2. Make sure that book or paper is sufficient distance from the edge of the desk to enable most/all of the forearm to rest on the desk. Move book up as child works down the page to maintain this.
3. Table or desk height about level with child's waistline or a bit higher. The weight of the body is supported by the non-writing arm.
4. Sloping desks are ideal, especially for struggling writers.
5. Feet should touch the floor (use a telephone book if needed).

Left-handers

Left-handers should have their elbow in to discourage a hooked wrist.

Posture rhyme:

1, 2, 3, 4. Are your feet flat on the floor?
5, 6, 7, 8. Is your back nice and straight?
9, 10, 11, 12. Show me how your pencil's held.
13, 14, 15, 16. Now it's time to do some writing.

GENERAL TEACHING TIPS

- Purchase extra copies of *Write for Queensland*—Prep and Book 1 to laminate for non-permanent marker use, allowing incidental, all-year reinforcement of handwriting lessons.
- Display the alphabet in lower-case and upper-case forms across the top of the board.
- Always commence writing lessons with finger exercises, incorporating rhymes, such as "Twinkle, Twinkle, Little Star", or "One Day My Thumb Was Moving", or games such as finger Olympics, mock piano playing, spider on a mirror, etc.
- Utilise old verbal letter cues to assist with direction, e.g. letter "b" like a bat and a ball: down for the bat and up and around for the ball.
- Modelling on the board or an overhead screen one letter at a time, and writing large letters in the air as a class, assists direction also.
- Slope is developmental and should be encouraged, but not enforced, at this stage.
- Felt pens/textas are ideal for pre-writing. Soft HB pencils (unpainted) are recommended for later stages.

Please see further information on the learning features of this book on page 3, and Teacher's Notes on page 63.

LEARNING FEATURES

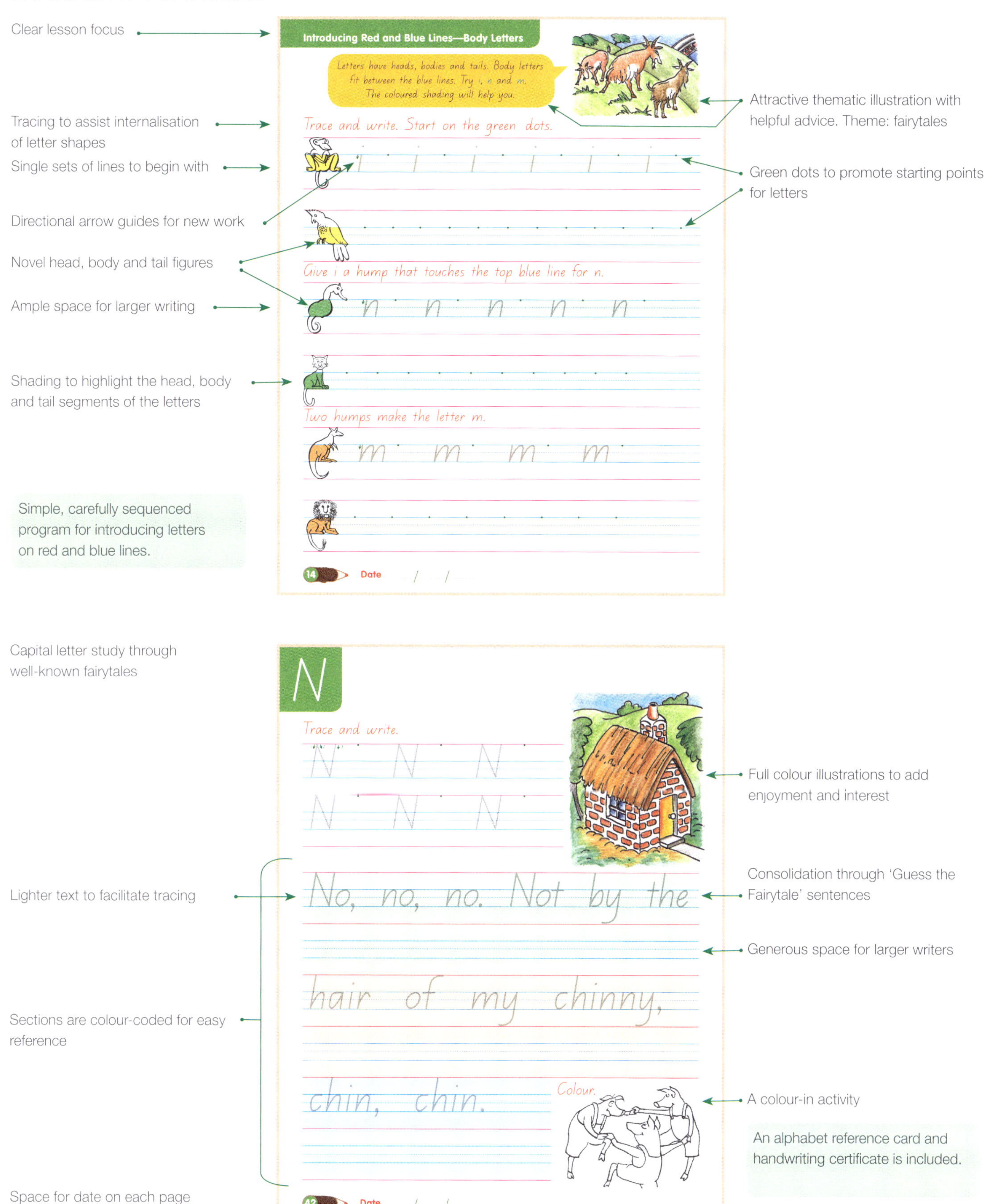

Trace the strings.
Draw more.
Start on the
green dots.

Trace the railings.
Draw more.

Trace the train track. Draw more.

Trace and write. Start on the green dots.

Date ..../........../..........

Trace and continue the pattern.

m m

Finish the pattern on the turtle shell.

Put more scales on the fish.

Trace and write. Start on the green dots.

r r r

n n n

h h h

m m m

Date ..../........../..........

Trace and continue the pattern. Start on the green dots.

m m

Draw blades on the scissors.

Give each cat a tail.

Trace and write.

k k k

b b b

p p p

j j j

Trace and continue the pattern.

m m

Make a jelly and pineapples using the m shape.

A wedge is the space in a letter that looks like a triangle.
Trace, write and colour the wedges.

n n n n

m m r r

h h k k

b b p p

Date ..../........../..........

Trace and continue the pattern. Start on the green dots.

uuu uuu

Put frills on Cinderella's dress. Use the u shape.

uuu

Draw more curls.

eee
eee

Trace and write.

u u u

v v v

w w w

o o o

e e e

 Date ..../........../..........

Trace and continue the pattern.

Give each soldier a flat shoulder.

Give each cat a tail.

Trace and write.

f f f

c c c

a a a

d d d

q q q

Trace and continue the pattern. Start on the green dots.

uu uu

Give the owls more feathers.

u
uu
uuu

Wedges on anti-clockwise letters are underneath.
Trace, write and colour the wedges.

u u u

w w w

a a a

q q q

d d d

Date ..../........../..........

Give each mouse a tail.

Give each butterfly two antennae.

Trace and write.

y y y

g g g

s s s

Date ....../....../......

Write more of letter c to finish the caterpillar.
Start on the green dots.

c c c c

c c c c

c c c c

Trace and write.
Circle the letters in your name.

a b c d e

f g h i j

k l m n o

p q r s t u

v w x y z

Date ..../........../..........

Draw more feathers on the peacocks.

Trace and write.

1 . 1 . 2 . 2 . 3 .

3 . 4 . 4 . 5 . 5 .

6 . 6 . 7 . 7 . 8 .

8 . 9 . 9 . 10 . . 10 . .

Date ..../......../........

Letters have heads, bodies and tails. Body letters fit between the blue lines. Try i, n and m. The coloured shading will help you.

Trace and write. Start on the green dots.

i i i i i i

Give i a hump that touches the top blue line for n.

n n n n n

Two humps make the letter m.

m m m m

Date ..../........../..........

Now try v, u and w.
The coloured shading will help you.

Trace and write. Start on the green dots.

v v v v v

u u u u u

w w w w

Body letters that start flat are c, a, s and z. The coloured shading will help you.

Trace and write. Start on the green dots.

c c c c c

a a a a a

s s s s s

Letter z starts from the left side.

z z z z z

Date ..../........../..........

Letter e is special.
It starts at the dotted line.
The coloured shading will help you.

Trace and write. Start on the green dots.

e e e e e

o o o o o

x x x x x

My body's nobody's body but mine.

Trace and write.

mouse worm

axe scissors

Date ..../........../..........

This is what I call body work!

Trace and write.

zoom cream

Cream

vase wave

Date .... / .... / ....

Body and tail letters
touch the bottom red line.
The coloured shading will help you.

Write i. Give it a tail to make j. Start on the green dots.

ij ij ij ij

Practise j.

Give u a tail to make y.

uy uy uy uy

Practise y.

Give a a tail to make g and q.

aq aq aq aq

Practise q.

Date ..../........./.........

Tails are not curly.
Another body and tail letter is p.
The coloured shading will help you.

Trace and write.

p p p

j j j

y y y

g g g

q q q

p p p

Date .... / .... / ....

Tails finish flat.

Trace and write.

jigsaw queen

popcorn garage

Date .... / .... / ....

Tails go down to the red line.

Trace and write.

goose pyjamas

yo-yo jump-rope

Date .... / .... / ....

Head and body letters
touch the top red line.
The coloured shading will help you.

Trace and write. Start on the green dots.

l l l l

h h h h

k k k k

Date ..../........../..........

Letter t is shorter than the other head and body letters. The coloured shading will help you.

Trace and write.

b b b b

Letter d starts on the top blue line.

d d d d

Letter f starts flat.

f f

Letter t is shorter.

t t

Date .... / .... / ....

Try some words that use body letters, body and tail letters, as well as head and body letters.

Trace and write.

telephone apple

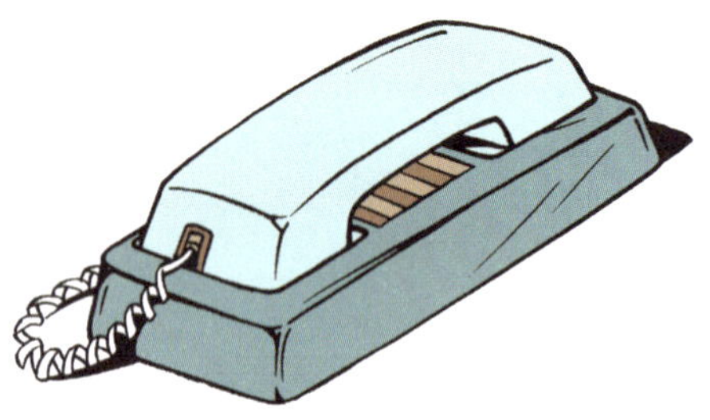

jacket chimney

Date ..../........../..........

Can I trick you?

Trace and write.

playtime light

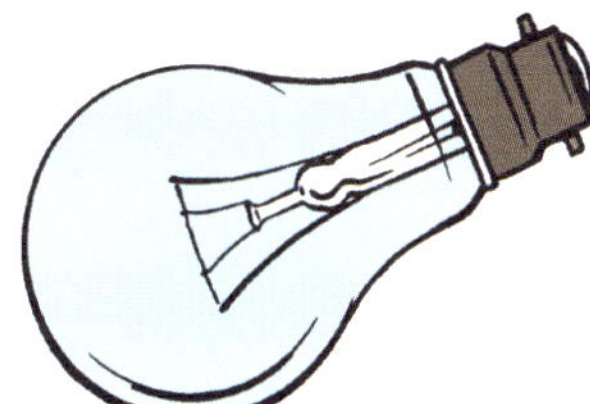

fishing monkey

Date .... / .... / ....

Numerals on Red and Blue Lines

Numerals are also written between the blue lines.
One crumb, two crumbs, three crumbs, four.

Trace and write. Start on the green dots.

0 0 1 1

2 2 3 3

4 4 5 5

6 6 7 7

8 or 8 8

9 9 10 10

Date ..../........../..........

Trace and write.

A A A

A A A

A great big forest grew around the castle.

Colour.

Date .... / .... / ....

B

Trace and write.

B B B

B B B

Being the fastest

is not always being

the best.

Colour.

Date ..../........../..........

c

Trace and write.

c c c

c c c

"Come with me," the

music said to all of

the children.

Colour.

D

Trace and write.

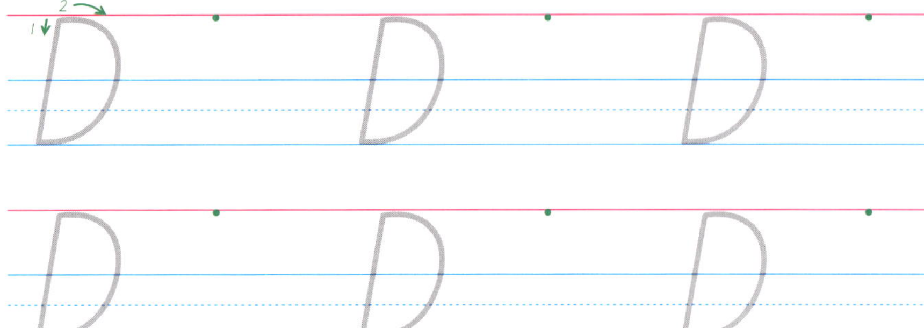

Don't stay past twelve

o'clock or the magic

will wear off.

Colour.

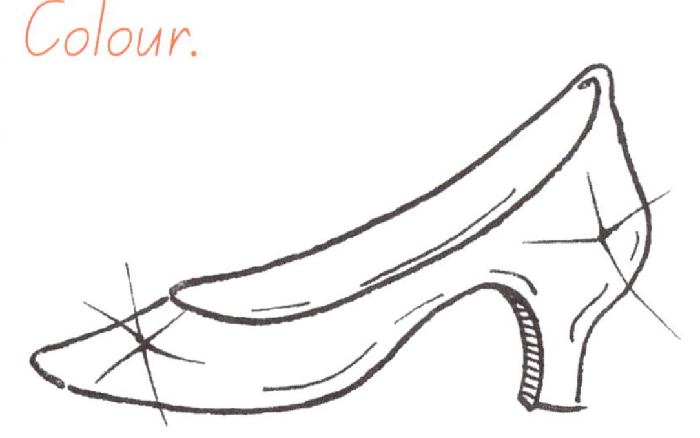

Date ..../........../..........

E

Trace and write.

E E E

E E E

Even as he spoke

his wooden nose

grew longer.

Colour.

F

Trace and write.

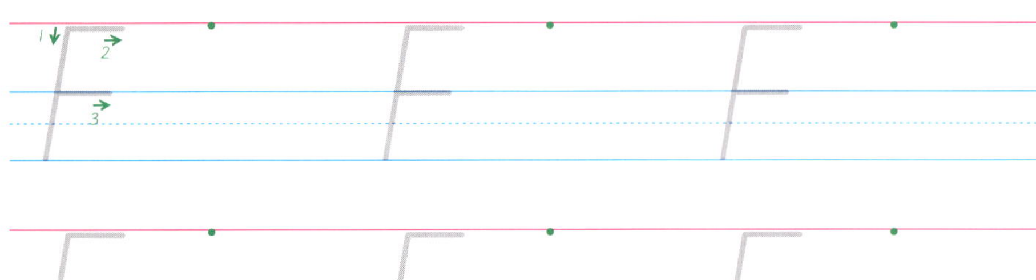

Fee, fi, fo, fum. I smell the blood of an Englishman.

Colour.

Date ..../........../..........

Trace and write.

G G G

G G G

Go away. Our mum

hasn't got black feet

like you.

Colour.

Date .... / .... / ....

Trace and write.

H H H

H H H

"Help, help!" But the

villagers did not

believe him.

Colour.

Date ..../........./.........

I THINK I CAN...

Trace and write.

I I I

I I I

I think I can. I

think I can. I think

I can.

Colour.

Date ....../....../......

J

Trace and write.

J J J

J J J

Just drink it and

your tail will split

into two legs.

Colour.

Date ..../........../..........

Trace and write.

K K K

K K K

Kiss me and I will

turn into a handsome

young prince.

Colour.

Date .... / .... / ....

L

Trace and write.

L L L

L L L

"Let down your hair,"

called the witch to

the tower.

Colour.

Date ..../........../..........

Trace and write.

M M

M M

Mirror, mirror on the

wall, who's the fairest

of them all?

Colour.

N

Trace and write.

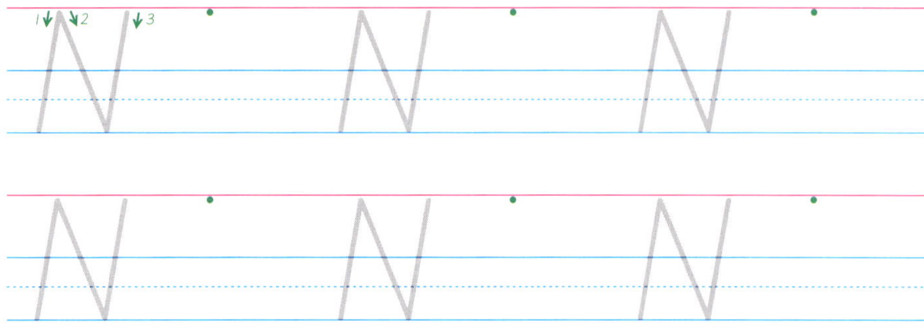

No, no, no. Not by the hair of my chinny, chin, chin.

Colour.

Date ..../........../..........

Trace and write.

One more bucket

went into the tub.

"Stop, stop!"

Colour.

p

Trace and write.

p p p

p p p

Poke out your finger

so I can feel how

fat you are.

Colour.

Date ..../........../..........

Trace and write.

Quick! The sky is

falling. I must tell

the king.

Colour.

Date .... / .... / ....

R

Trace and write.

R R R

R R R

Run, run, as fast as

you can. You can't

catch me.

Colour.

Date ..../........../..........

Trace and write.

S S S

S S S

Someone's been sitting

in my chair and

broken it.

Colour.

Date ...... / ...... / ......

T

Trace and write.

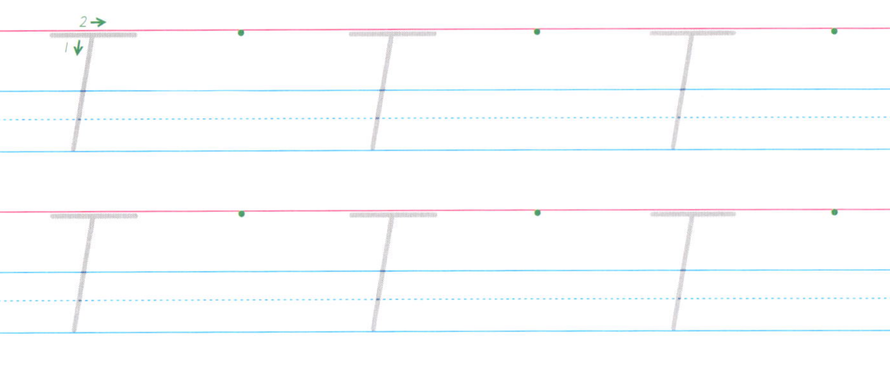

Then I shall take the wheat to the mill myself.

Colour.

 Date ..../........./.........

Trace and write.

U U U

U U U

Under the mattresses

the queen put one

dried pea.

Colour.

Date ...... / ...... / ......

V

Trace and write.

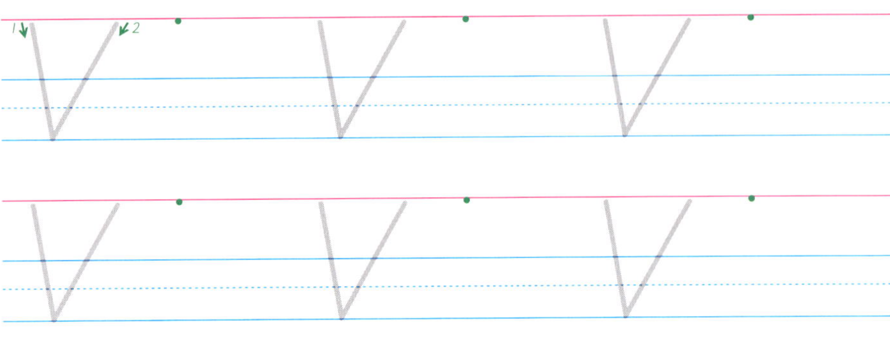

Very well. Go across the bridge to the green grass.

Colour.

Date ..../........./.........

Trace and write.

W W
W W

"What big ears you have, Grandma," said the girl.

Colour.

Date ....../....../......

X

Trace and write.

X X X

X X X

Let me go, please.

One day you may

need my help.

Colour.

Date ....../....../......

Trace and write.

Y Y Y

Y Y Y

You will become an

ugly beast until you

find a wife.

Colour.

Z

Trace and write.

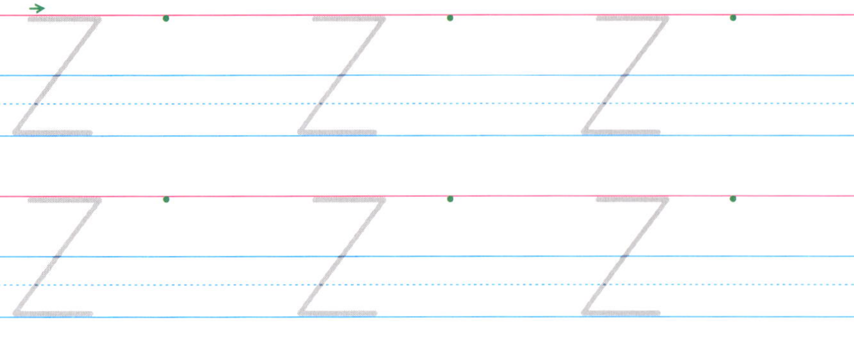

"Is your name Ziggy,

Zander or Zachary?"

"Not, it is not."

Colour.

Date ..../........../..........

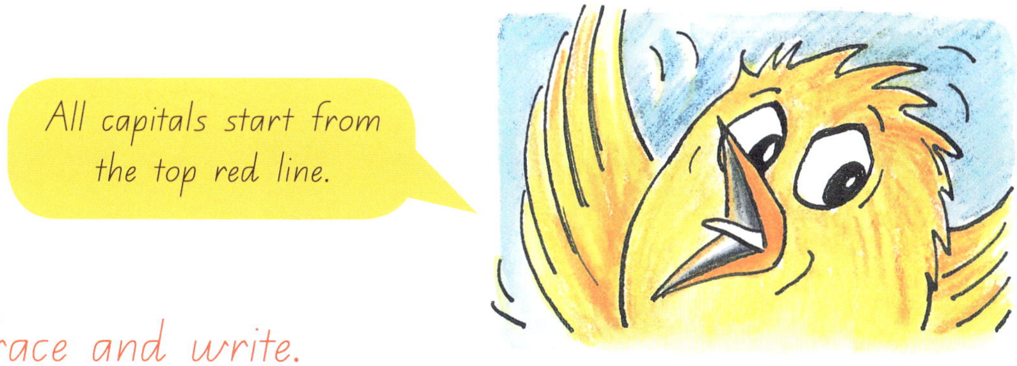
All capitals start from the top red line.

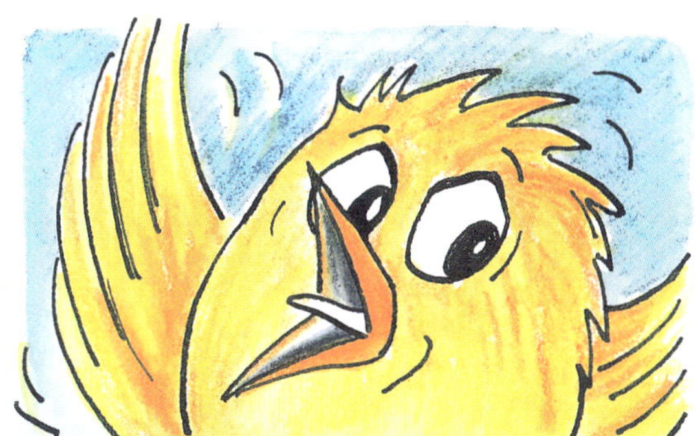

Trace and write.

STOP GO ON OFF

DANGER EXIT

HOT COLD NEWS

OFFICE LIBRARY

Date .... / .... / ....

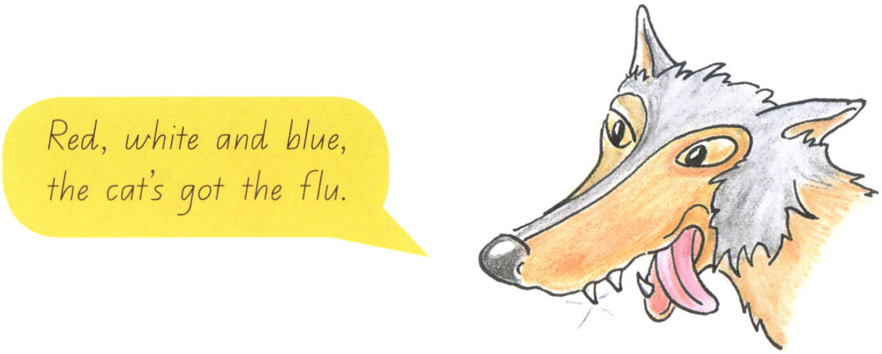
Red, white and blue,
the cat's got the flu.

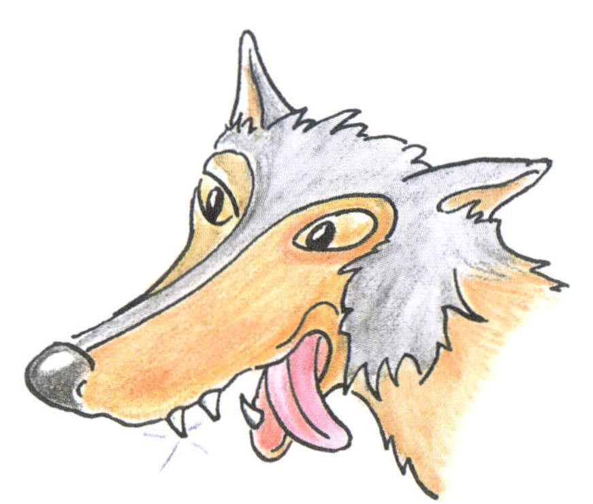

Trace and write.

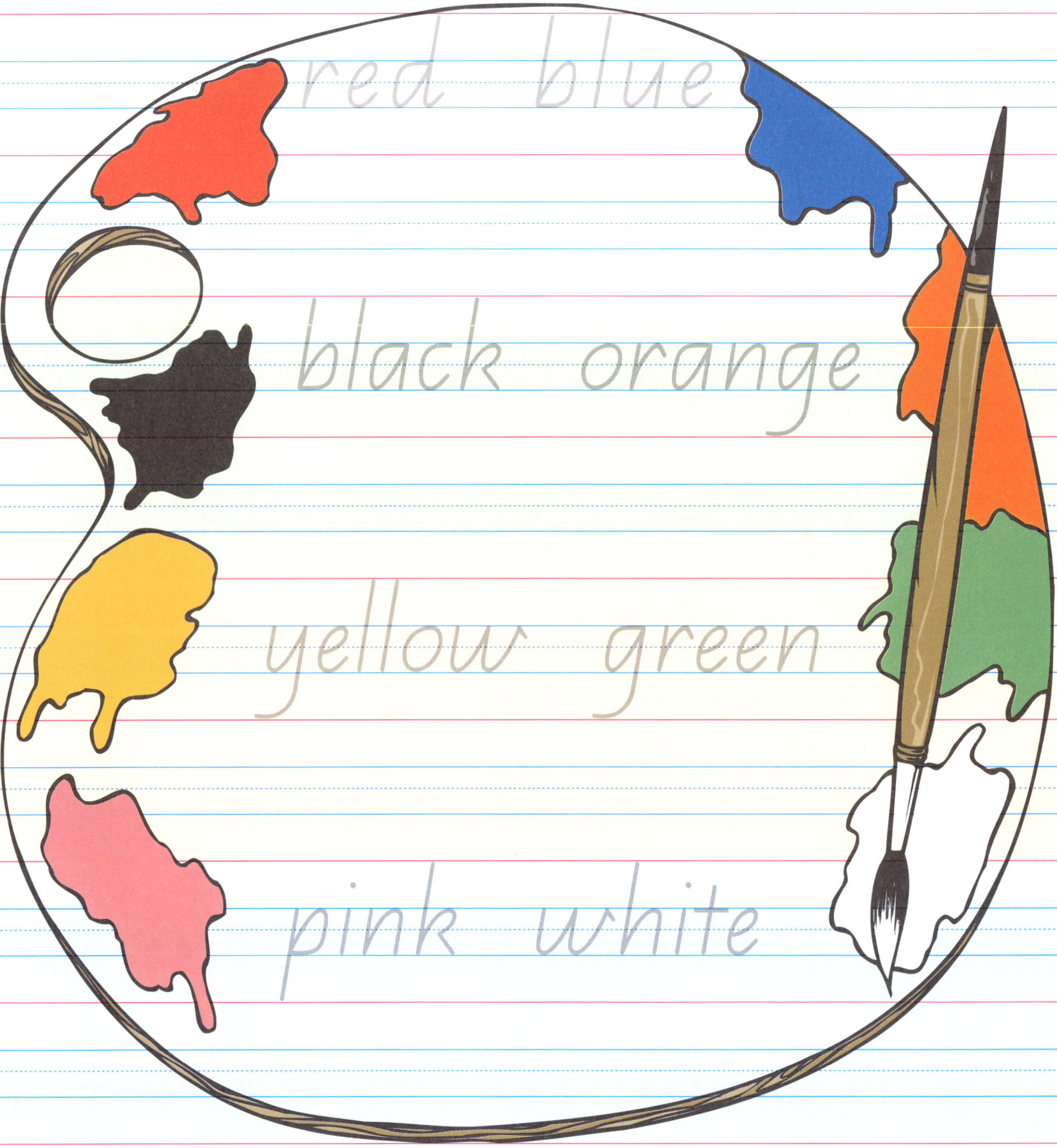
red blue
black orange
yellow green
pink white

Date ..../........../..........

Old Mother Ink
Fell down the sink.
How many cupfuls
Did she drink?

Match the number words to the numerals.

5 12 9 2 3 11 8 1 7 10 4 6

one two three

four five six

seven eight nine

ten eleven twelve

Date .... / .... / ....

Read "Pat the Cat", "Jen the Hen", "Mig the Pig", "Tog the Dog" and "Zug the Bug", all by Colin and Jacqui Hawkins.

Trace and write.

hat rat bat sat

men pen hen ten

big wig tig fig

dog log rug jug

Date ..../........../..........

Read "Elmer" by David McKee.

Decorate the elephants using four patterns.

stripes  dots

checks  swirls

zig-zags  hearts

stars  crosses

Date ..../......../........

Read "Dear Zoo" by Rod Campbell.

Finish the page for "Dear Seaworld".

Please send me a pet.

They sent me a ________.

He was too ____________.

I sent him back.

Date ..../........./.........

January

Eachie, peachie,
pear, plum,
When does your
birthday come?

Trace and write.

February March April

May June July August

September October

November December

Circle your birthday month.

Date ..../........../..........

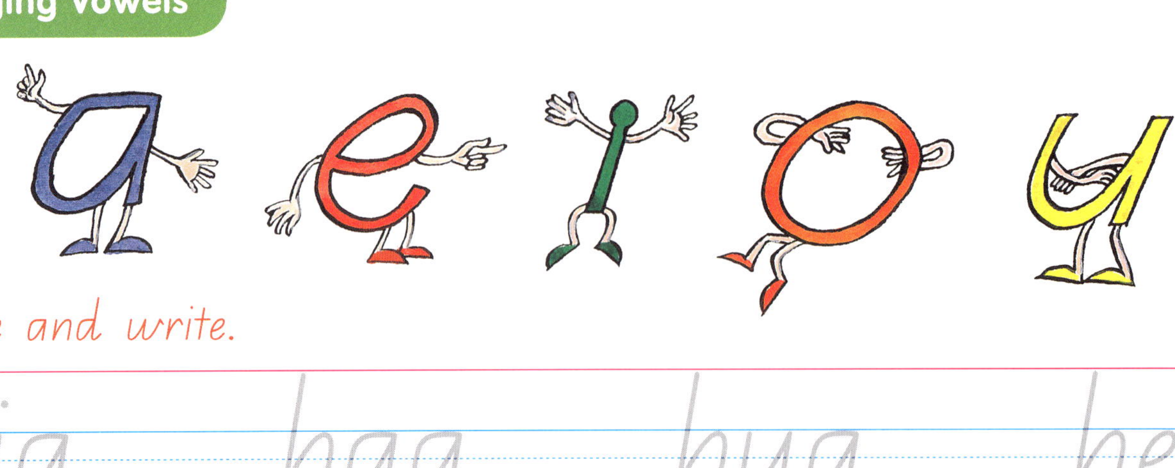

Trace and write.

big bag bug beg

pig peg cot cut

cat fun fin fan

ball bell bull bill

Date ..../........../..........

TEACHER'S NOTES

Page

1 Title page and list of contents. The student writes his/her name. Missing letters may be filled in after pages 4 to 11 are completed.

2 Introduction

3 Learning Features

4 Letters are introduced according to directional rotation on base lines. Starting arrows indicate where letter commences, as well as its direction. Starting dots for letters ensure even spacing. Strokes are numbered when lifting for crossbars. Slope is developmental and should be talked about and encouraged.

5–7 This clockwise pattern can be called the "three-mountain pattern". It is useful for developing the rhythm and flow of handwriting. It has been lengthened in some pre-writing patterns to four or more, but mostly only three, as this is ideal for allowing the correct shape and allowing the hand to move across the page. Practise in the air. Letter "r" is a narrow letter.

6 While some beginning writers prefer to lift the pencil when writing "p" (and later "d"), they will develop into more fluent writers if this letter is written in one movement, retracing "back up the pole". Letters "b", "p" and "j" finish with a flat shoulder, not a fish-hook/umbrella-handle shape.

7 A wedge is the gap between the downstroke and the upstroke. For ease of instruction, wedges start halfway (they are actually a little larger), and may be likened to a triangle of cheese. Wedges may be coloured in.

8 Letter "o" starts at the top, in the middle; "e" is one of the two letters that do not start at the top of their shape (the other being "d"), it goes upwards from its middle and is very narrow. Tails on "v" and "w" are best kept short.

8–10 This anti-clockwise pattern can be called the "three-scoop pattern". The running writing "e" pattern, likewise, usually has three loops, but can be longer. Practise in the air.

9 These anti-clockwise letters start with a flat shoulder commencing on the line—no fish-hook or umbrella handles! Note that "d" has the same starting point as "a" with no pencil lift (see note for page 6). "d" finishes with a tail, or cursive exit, to minimise the "b"–"d" confusion. "q" finishes with a short point.

11–12 Letters with both movements will need lots of practising "in the air".

13 In Queensland, "8" may be written as an open or closed numeral. Both commence in the same place.

14–17 Instruction begins on 8 mm red and blue lines, according to spatial groups. The shaded area of the animals is a guide to the lines/space used. BODY LETTERS fit between the blue lines, all starting on the top blue line, except for "e", which starts on the dotted line in the middle. One or two humps are added to the downstroke of the letter "i" (without lifting) for easy progression to "n" and "m". Wedges may be shaded on this and any of the following pages. **Note** that across pages 14 to 28, shading indicates the areas of the lines that the letters will be formed in (head, body, tail).

18–19 Words—Most value will come from tracing if each letter is traced in sequence.

20–21 BODY AND TAIL LETTERS—"j", "y", "g" and "q" are introduced as an extension of an appropriate body letter. The shaded area of the animals is a guide to the lines/spaces used. Remember that tails finish flat along the red line, except for "q" which has a short point.

22–23 Letter "p" should be completed without a pencil lift (see note for page 6). Words—Most value will come from tracing if each letter is traced in sequence.

24 HEAD AND BODY LETTERS—Start on the top red line. The shaded area of the animals is a guide to the lines/spaces used.

25 Letter "d" starts on the top blue line as for letter "a", with no lifting (see notes for pages 6 and 9). Letter "t" starts halfway between the top red line and the top blue line, to help tell it apart from "l" in cursive.

26–27 Words—Most value will come from tracing if each letter is traced in sequence.

28 Except for "9", numerals do not generally reflect alphabet shapes.

29–55 CAPITALS—These are all head and body letters. As a suggested introduction for each capital, first read the story listed below. **Note** that across pages 29 to 62 all areas of the lines are shaded because head, body and tail letters occur across all these pages. Each line of text is shaded differently to allow teachers to easily instruct children as they work down each page.

29–54 Guess the fairytale using sentence context and picture clues.

29 Fairytale: Sleeping Beauty

30 Fairytale: The Hare and the Tortoise

31 Fairytale: The Pied Piper

32 Fairytale: Cinderella

33 Fairytale: Pinocchio

34 Fairytale: Jack and the Beanstalk

35 Fairytale: The Wolf and the Seven Kids

36 Fairytale: The Boy Who Cried Wolf

37 Fairytale: The Little Engine

38 Fairytale: The Little Mermaid

39 Fairytale: The Frog Prince

40 Fairytale: Rapunzel

41 Fairytale: Snow White

42 Fairytale: The Three Little Pigs

43 Fairytale: The Sorcerer's Apprentice

44 Fairytale: Hansel and Gretel

45 Fairytale: Chicken Little

46 Fairytale: The Gingerbread Man

47 Fairytale: Goldilocks and the Three Bears

48 Fairytale: The Little Red Hen

49 Fairytale: The Princess and the Pea

50 Fairytale: The Three Billy Goats Gruff

51 Fairytale: Little Red Riding Hood

52 Fairytale: The Lion and the Mouse

53 Fairytale: Beauty and the Beast

54 Fairytale: Rumpelstiltskin

55 Words commonly seen in all-capitals.

56 Colour Words

57 Number Words

58 Rhyming Words

59 Pattern Words

60 Animal Words

61 Calendar Words

62 Changing Vowels

63 Teacher's Notes

64 Certificate

Inside back cover — Reference Card—May be detached and contacted to the student's desk.

Congratulations!
writes the letters
of the alphabet
neatly and
correctly.
Teacher:
Date: